curious about

DROUGHTS

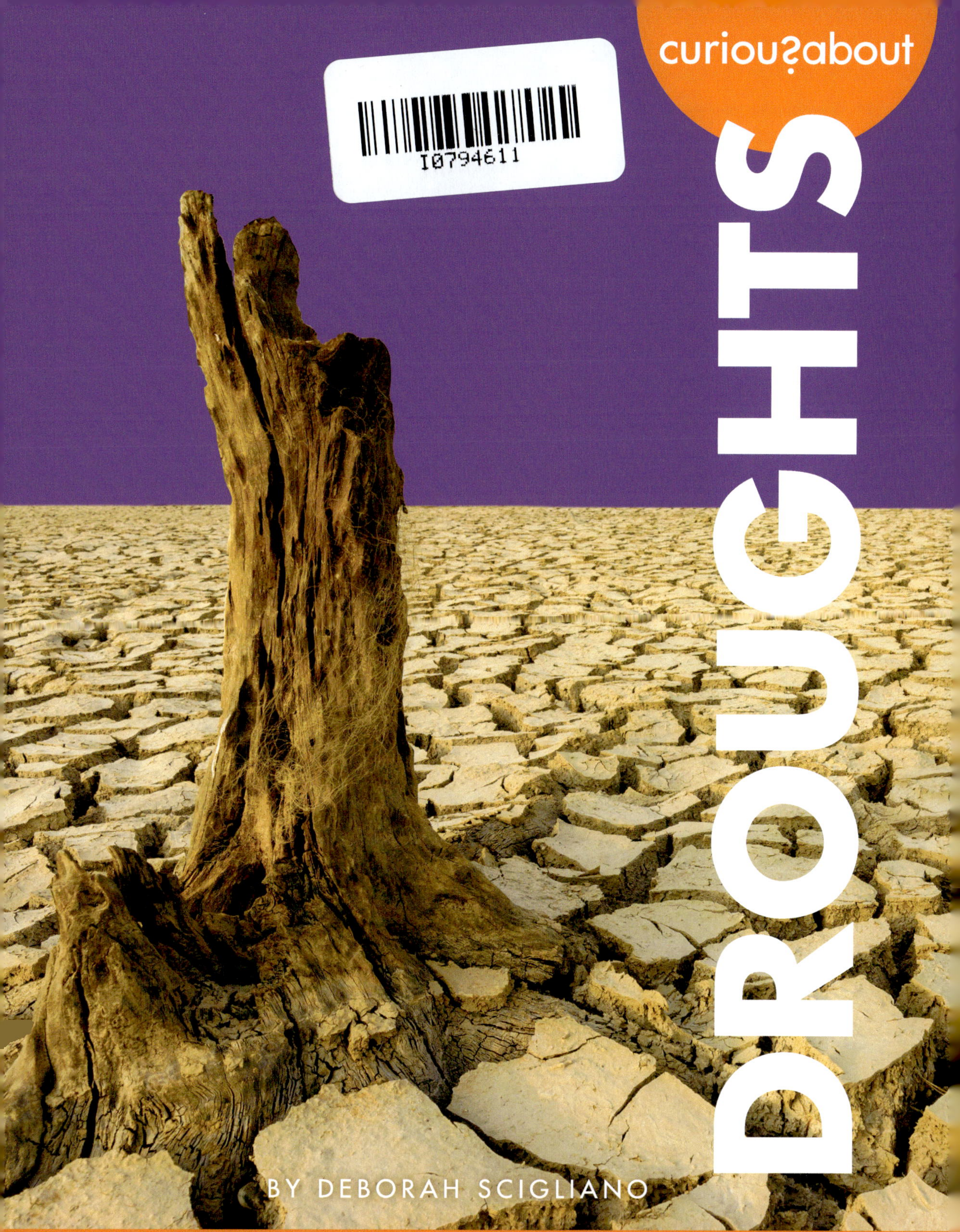

BY DEBORAH SCIGLIANO

AMICUS LEARNING

What are you

curious about?

CHAPTER THREE

A Long Dry Time

Curious About is published by
Amicus Learning, an imprint of Amicus
P.O. Box 227, Mankato, MN 56002
www.amicuspublishing.us

Editor: Ana Brauer
Series Designer: Kathleen Petelinsek
Book Designer and Photo Researcher: Kathleen Petelinsek

Library of Congress Cataloging-in-Publication Data
Names: Scigliano, Deborah A., 1951– author
Title: Curious about droughts / by Deborah Scigliano.
Description: Mankato, MN : Amicus Learning, an imprint of Amicus, [2026] | Series: Curious about extreme weather | Includes bibliographical references and index. | Audience: Ages 6–9 | Audience: Grades 2–3 | Summary: "What was the longest drought? Learn the causes and effects of droughts in this question-and-answer book for elementary-aged readers. Includes infographics, table of contents, glossary, books and websites for further research, and index"— Provided by publisher.
Identifiers: LCCN 2025011936 (print) | LCCN 2025011937 (ebook) | ISBN 9798892008365 library binding | ISBN 9798892009027 paperback | ISBN 9798892009683 ebook
Subjects: LCSH: Droughts—Juvenile literature
Classification: LCC QC929.25 .S387 2026 (print) | LCC QC929.25 (ebook) | DDC 551.57/73—dc23/eng/20250604
LC record available at https://lccn.loc.gov/2025011936
LC ebook record available at https://lccn.loc.gov/2025011937

Photo Credits: Shutterstock/Aaron Myrtle, 2, 12, AlbertoGonzalez, 4–5, Chris Ison, 19 (second from bottom), Droneandy, 2, 9, emka angelina, 22, 23, J.J. Gouin, 20-21, KITTIPONG SOMKLANG, cover, 1, Piyaset, 10–11, Ramsey Samara, 19 (bottom), Realphotos83, 18, Sirius3001, 13; Wikimedia Commons/Book of Alberto Decombe, 19 (top), Contains modified Copernicus Sentinel data 2022, 15, Dorothea Lange, 3, 16–17, Ibrahimassoumane, 19 (middle), NOAA George E. Marsh Album, 19 (second from top)

CHAPTER ONE

What is a drought?

A drought can make lakes dry up.

It is a dry time that goes on for months or years. There is little or no rain. Water levels begin to drop. The soil becomes extremely dry. It happens slowly. A drought can last for a long time.

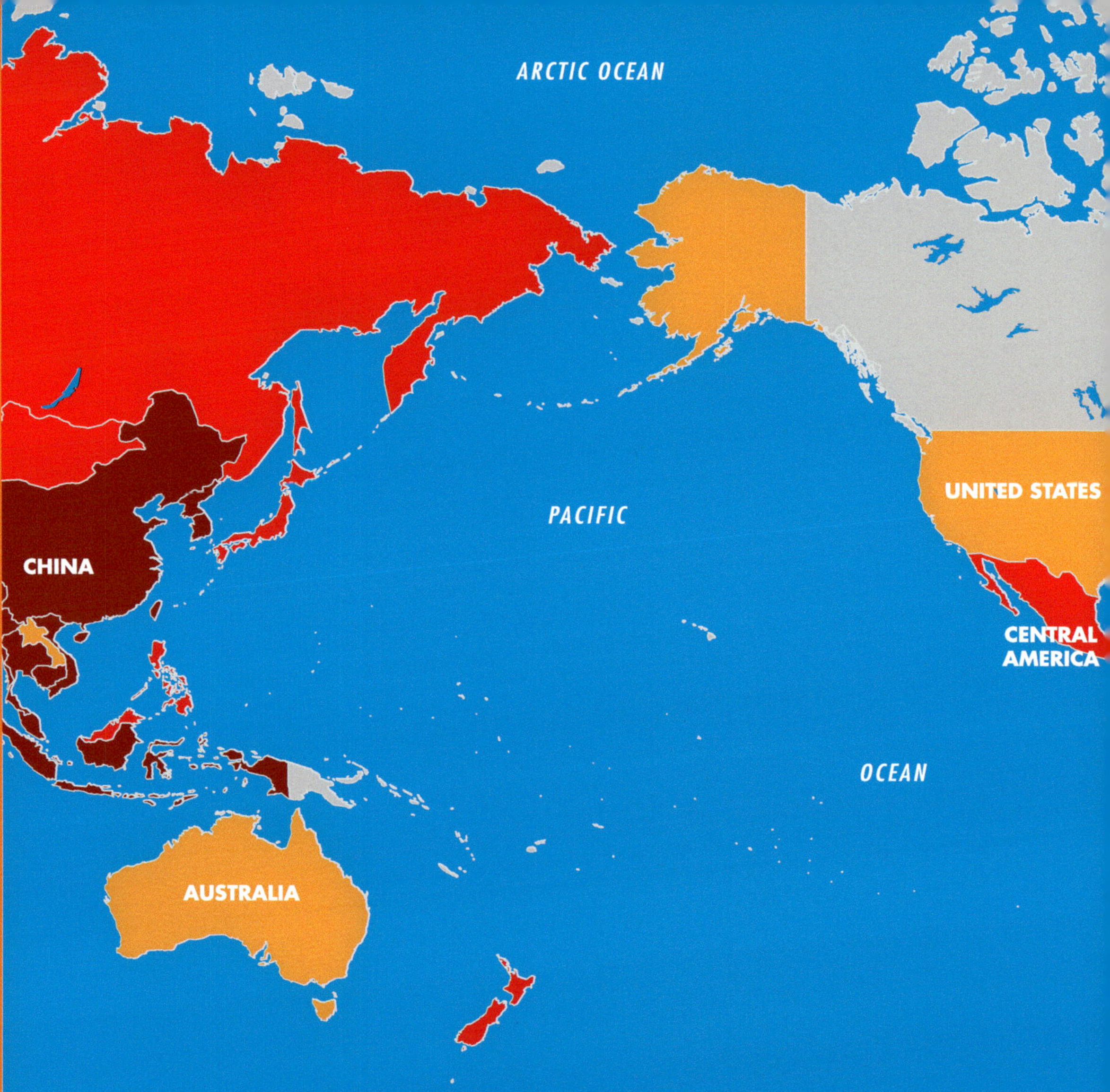

Where do droughts happen?

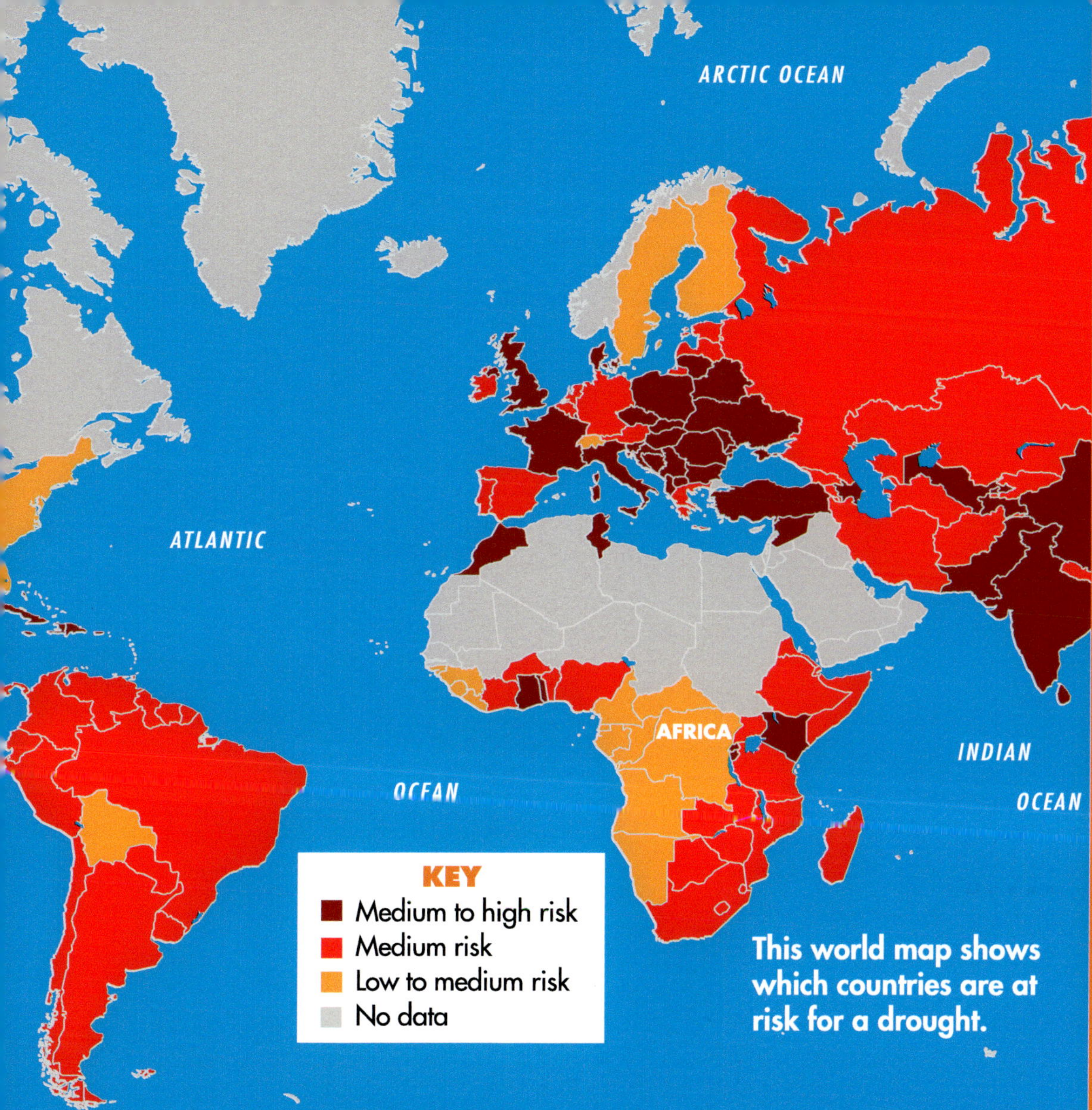

This world map shows which countries are at risk for a drought.

All over the world. They happen in dry areas. Parts of Africa, China, and Central America have frequent droughts. The western United States and Australia have them, too. Some can be very severe. Water sources dry up. Crops die. People may experience **famine**.

When do droughts start?

It can be hard to tell. They happen so slowly. Rainfall amount is one way to tell. A lack of rain causes a dry spell. Dry spells can turn into droughts when they last longer than a few weeks. The soil dryness is another way to tell.

A drought causes plants to dry up and die.

CHAPTER TWO

What causes a drought?

DID YOU KNOW?
Heat waves can cause droughts and droughts can cause heat waves.

There are many causes. **Climate change** is a big cause. Places become hotter. Water **evaporates** faster when it is hot. Wind changes can also cause one. Wind moves clouds. Clouds bring needed rain. No clouds mean no rain.

A drought makes the temperature rise quickly.

What happens during a drought?

Droughts make it hard for animals to find food.

Droughts affect people, animals, and plants. The dryness can lead to wildfires. Animals can lose their habitats. Crops dry up. **Dust storms** can happen. Water becomes scarce. People may not have enough to eat.

A dust storm can make it hard to see when you are driving.

How do you know when one happens?

Scientists use **satellites** to track dry conditions around the world. Rainfall, river levels, soil moisture, and temperature help scientists find droughts. The North American Drought Monitor shows where droughts are in the US, Canada, and Mexico.

DROUGHT CATEGORIES

D1 Moderate
D2 Severe
D3 Extreme
D4 Exceptional

These satellite pictures show how much the Amazon River's water goes down during a drought.

September 29, 2022

September 29, 2023

The Dust Bowl was one of the longest and worst droughts in US history.

How long does a drought last?

They can last weeks or months. Some even last years. Scientists **classify** droughts into short and long ones. A long drought lasts longer than six months. A long drought happened in the United States in 1930. It lasted about 10 years. It was named The Dust Bowl. Around 7,000 people died.

What is the longest drought?

Rain is very rare in Arica, Chile.

Arica, Chile has the longest one on record. It lasted from October 1903 to January 1918. That's more than 14 years! Arica is considered the driest city in the world. It gets an average 0.03 inches (0.8 millimeters) of rain per year.

ARICA, CHILE
1903–1918

DUST BOWL, UNITED STATES
1930–1939

SAHEL REGION, AFRICA
1968–EARLY 1980s

SOUTHERN AUSTRALIA
1997–2009

CALIFORNIA, UNITED STATES
2011–2017

Can I prepare for a drought?

DID YOU KNOW?

You can catch rainwater in a container. This water can be used in the garden. It can also be treated and made safe to drink.

Yes! You can start by helping **conserve** water. Turning off the water while you brush your teeth helps. This can save 8 gallons (30 liters) of water each time. Taking short, five-minute showers helps, too!

Rainwater can be helpful when you save it.

STAY CURIOUS!

ASK MORE QUESTIONS

How do satellites help find droughts?

Has a drought happened where I live?

Try a BIG QUESTION:
Can water be sent to drought areas?

SEARCH FOR ANSWERS

Search the library catalog or the Internet.
A librarian, teacher, or parent can help you.

Using Keywords
Find the looking glass.

Keywords are the most important words in your question.

If you want to know about:

- how satellites monitor droughts, type: SATELLITES AND DROUGHTS
- droughts near me, type: DROUGHTS IN (YOUR STATE)

LEARN MORE

FIND GOOD SOURCES

Here are some good, safe sources you can use in your research.
Your librarian can help you find more.

Books

Curious about Saving Water
by Amy Hansen, 2025.

Dangerous Droughts
by Lola Schaefer, 2022.

Internet Sites

Drought for Kids
https://drought.unl.edu/Education/DroughtforKids.aspx
Learn more about droughts, the people who study them, the impact on us, and more.

Dust Bowl
https://kids.britannica.com/kids/article/Dust-Bowl/390020
Find out about the worst drought in United States history – the Dust Bowl.

Every effort has been made to ensure that these websites are appropriate for children. However, because of the nature of the Internet, it's impossible to guarantee that these sites will remain active indefinitely or that their contents will not be altered.

SHARE AND TAKE ACTION

Take a shorter shower.
Five minutes or less can save gallons (liters) of water each time.

Go to the library and read more books about droughts.
Learn more about droughts and how they happen.

Create a *Ways to Conserve Water* poster.
Use ideas for conserving water to design a poster. Share this with your family.

GLOSSARY

conserve To use in amounts that are no more than necessary to avoid waste.

classify To sort into groups.

climate change Changes in the Earth's weather patterns.

dust storm Wind blows dry, loose soil through the air making it hard to see and breathe.

evaporate To pass off or cause to pass off into vapor from a liquid state.

famine An extreme lack of food that can lead to hunger and starvation.

satellite A spacecraft that is sent into orbit around a planet to gather and send back information.

INDEX

About the Author

Deborah Scigliano is an educator and a writer. She has taught elementary students and college students. She loves to write for children. Science, especially weather, is a special interest of hers.